D1552248

Building Character

Being Tolerant

by Penelope S. Nelson

Bullfrog
Books

Ideas for Parents and Teachers

Bullfrog Books let children practice reading informational text at the earliest reading levels. Repetition, familiar words, and photo labels support early readers.

Before Reading

- Discuss the cover photo. What does it tell them?
- Look at the picture glossary together. Read and discuss the words.

Read the Book

- "Walk" through the book and look at the photos. Let the child ask questions. Point out the photo labels.
- Read the book to the child, or have him or her read independently.

After Reading

- Prompt the child to think more. Ask: There are many ways to show tolerance. How can you show tolerance today?

Bullfrog Books are published by Jump!
5357 Penn Avenue South
Minneapolis, MN 55419
www.jumplibrary.com

Library of Congress Cataloging-in-Publication Data

Names: Nelson, Penelope, 1994– author.
Title: Being tolerant / by Penelope S. Nelson.
Description: Minneapolis, MN: Jump!, Inc., [2020]
Series: Building character
Includes bibliographical references and index.
Identifiers: LCCN 2018050111 (print)
LCCN 2018058143 (ebook)
ISBN 9781641287166 (ebook)
ISBN 9781641287142 (hardcover: alk. paper)
ISBN 9781641287159 (paperback)
Subjects: LCSH: Toleration. Classification: LCC HM1271 (ebook) | LCC HM1271 .N485 2020 (print)
DDC 179/.9—dc23
LC record available at https://lccn.loc.gov/2018050111

Editor: Jenna Trnka
Designer: Michelle Sonnek

Photo Credits: annebaek/iStock, cover; FatCamera/iStock, 1, 8–9 (foreground); Elena Blokhina/Shutterstock, 3; Robert Kneschke/Shutterstock, 4; wavebreakmedia/Shutterstock, 5, 20–21, 23tl; Laboo Studio/Shutterstock, 6–7 (left), 23br; Gelpi/Shutterstock, 6–7 (right), 23br; ImageFlow/Shutterstock, 6–7 (background), 23br; Arne Beruldsen/Shutterstock, 8–9 (background); Richard Hutchings/Getty, 10–11; MAHATHIR MOHD YASIN/Shutterstock, 12; Juanmonino/iStock, 13; PeopleImages/iStock, 14–15, 23bl; focal point/Shutterstock, 16; Lisa F. Young/Shutterstock, 17, 23tr; StockImageFactory.com/Shutterstock, 18–19; Mikael Damkier/Shutterstock, 22 (left); Lisa F. Young/Shutterstock, 22 (middle); LiliGraphie/Shutterstock, 22 (right); Gelpi/Shutterstock, 24.

Printed in the United States of America at Corporate Graphics in North Mankato, Minnesota.

Table of Contents

Kind to All

Let's be tolerant! How?

We accept everyone.

Even when we are not the same.

We are kind.

5

Jill and Pat dress differently.
They are still friends.

Owen is new
on the team.

Jona helps him.

He is patient.

wheelchair

Tim uses a wheelchair.

Jo helps him.

They go to school.

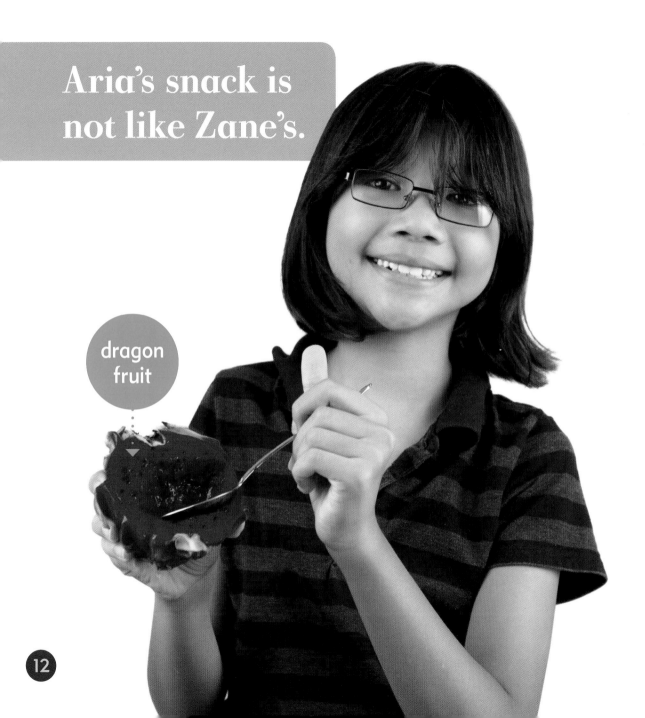

Aria's snack is not like Zane's.

dragon fruit

Zane asks her about it.

He is nice.

He learns.

Neat!

apple

13

Trin is patient.

She helps her little sister.

She helps grandma, too!

Liz and Eli celebrate different holidays.

They teach each other about them.

Cool!

Mack and Meg don't like the same things.

They want to watch different movies.

But they listen.

They decide to watch both.

Nice!

Be kind.

Learn about something new!

Celebrate a New Holiday!

Different people celebrate different holidays. Do you have a friend who celebrates a holiday that you don't? Learn about it! Ask him or her about it. Check out a book from the library. Have an adult help you learn more online.

When is the holiday? Are there special foods they eat? Do they exchange gifts? Or have other special traditions? How did the holiday start?

Picture Glossary

accept
To approve of someone without judgment and without wanting to change that person.

celebrate
To do something special to mark a special occasion or holiday.

patient
Able to accept delays or problems without getting angry or upset.

tolerant
Willing to respect or accept the customs, beliefs, or opinions of others.

Index

To Learn More

Finding more information is as easy as 1, 2, 3.

❶ Go to www.factsurfer.com

❷ Enter "beingtolerant" into the search box.

❸ Click the "Surf" button to see a list of websites.